ALL TIME HEROES

FROM ALL TIMES

~ Volume 3 ~

All Time Heroes

from All Times

~ Volume 3 ~

The Martyrdom of
Saint George of Cappadocia

ST SHENOUDA'S MONASTERY
SYDNEY, AUSTRALIA
2014

All Time Heroes From All Times - Volume 3
The Martyrdom of Saint George of Cappadocia

ST SHENOUDA MONASTERY
8419 Putty Rd,
Putty, NSW, 2330
Sydney, Australia

www.stshenoudamonastery.org.au

ISBN 13: 978-0-9873400-9-2

Cover Design:
Hani Ghaly,
Begoury Graphics
begourygraphics@gmail.com

CONTENTS

THE MARTYRDOM OF SAINT GEORGE   7

THE ENCOMIUM BY SAINT THEODOSIUS   39

THE MIRACLES OF SAINT GEORGE   45

THE MARTYRDOM OF SAINT GEORGE

In the Name of God...

The martyrdom of Saint George, the valiant martyr of our Lord Jesus Christ, who completed his strife on the 23rd of Pharmuthi, in the peace of God. Amen.

There was a time when a severe and terrible storm of persecution came upon the Church. In all cities, governors worshipped devilish idols and they compelled the preachers of truth to worship idols with them. There was a certain governor called Dadianus, who acquired dominion over the four quarters of the earth. When Dadianus became chief, he sat on the tribune and wrote edicts to be proclaimed throughout the whole world.

In the edict, he would say: "A rumour has spread that He to whom Mary gave birth and to whom the Jews slew, is the God who alone is to be worshipped. This means that Apollo, Poseidon, Hermes, Astarte, Zeus, Ezabel, Uranus, Scamandros and all the other gods are not to be worshipped. Therefore I write to every place and to the governors and authorities of every land and I declare that they speedily gather to meet me, so as to know the decision of my power."

Consequently, seventy governors from all parts of the world and great multitudes of people, gathered to meet Dadianus. Dadianus brought out all the instruments of the torture chamber and lay them before the multitudes. There were instruments of all sorts; the brazen bed, the bone smashing choppers, the iron rods, wheels with knives fixed to them, wooden horses, wooden gloves, iron gloves, tongue slitting knives, tools for drawing out teeth, the iron bone borer, sharp saws and other implements of cruel torture.

Dadianus then swore an oath, saying, "If I find anyone who refuses to worship the gods, I will torture them with bitter sufferings, I will smash their heads, I will cut out their brains with sharp knives, I will saw off their shin bones, I will tear open their bodies and I will cut off their limbs."

When the multitude heard these things, they feared the tortures greatly. Three years went by without anyone daring to say: "I am a Christian."

There was a young man named George, the sun of truth and the gloriois star between heaven and earth. He was a tribune in the imperial army and he came from Cappadocia. When he had served his time as tribune and acquired much wealth, he came to the governor Dadianus and wished to be made a count by him. When Saint George came to the city and saw the frenzied idolatry of the governors and how they had forsaken God, he immediately gave up his rank of tribune and said: "I will become a soldier of my Lord Jesus Christ, the King of heaven." After distributing his wealth to the poor, he rushed to the governors and cried out: "Cease your frenzy O governors for these idols are not gods. Let all your gods perish. As for me, I will worship one God, the Father of my Lord Jesus Christ and the Holy Spirit."

Dadianus then looked at Saint George and said: "Anyone who does not worship these gods will perish for our gods are mighty beings. You have not just despised us by what you said, but you have also despised the gods. Offer sacrifices to Apollo because he is the saviour of the whole world and be sure that the gods honour those who worship them and punish those who despise them. Know tell me, from where do you come, what is your name and why did you come here?"

Saint George answered and said: "The chief name which I bear is Christian. I am a Cappadocian and I was a soldier in a famous army. I performed my duties of tribune satisfactorily in Palestine. Now, who are these gods whom you want me to worship, O king?"

The governor said to him: "I want you to worship Apollo who hung out the heavens and Poseidon who made fast the earth."

Saint George replied: "O evil dragon, these are not gods and for the sake of these multitudes I will tell you who the righteous God is. Who do you want me to worship, O governor? Peter, the chosen of the Apostles or Apollo who corrupts the whole world. To whom should I offer sacrifice? To Elijah the Tishbite who was taken up to the gates of heaven or to Scamandros, the sorcerer who worked enchantments by fire, who committed adultery with Timetia and who begot Saar and Sarphat, whose deeds were evil and who were cast into the abyss of the sea? Tell me O king, to which of these would you give judgement...To Samuel who prayed to God or to Poseidon, the destroyer of ships in the sea? To Antaeus and

Herakles, or to the Martyrs and Prophets who wear crowns? Tell me O King, to which of these would you give judgement... To Jezebel, the slayer of the Prophets, or to Mary, the Virgin and Mother of God? Be ashamed, O king, for the things which you worship are not gods, but deaf idols."

When Saint George had said these things, the governor was greatly enraged and commanded them to hang him on a wooden horse and to torture him until his bowels fell out. After this, he was laid out and beaten with leather whips, until his body was torn in shreds. His wounds were sprinkled with salt. They brought hair sacks with which to excoriate his body until his blood ran like water; but St George remained patient amidst all these sufferings.

They brought iron boots with holes bred in them and they drove nails into the soles of his feet. Dadianus built a high platform and brought sixty sharp stakes to lacerate the body of St George. The saint was taken off the platform and put into a cauldron of boiled water. The soldiers beat his head with iron nails until they broke his skull and his brain poured out. His mouth was as white as lead and his body was congealed with blood. Eight soldiers rolled a heavy pillar onto the belly of Saint George.

The Lord appeared to Saint George during the night and told him: "Be strong and of good cheer, beloved George, for I will strengthen you to bear all the sufferings brought upon you. Among those born of woman, no one has arisen greater than John the Baptist and after him, there shall rise none like you. Behold, I have made you lord over seventy governors and whatever you say, shall happen to them. You shall die three times, but I will raise you up again. However, on the fourth time, I will come on a cloud and take you to the place of safe keeping. Be strong and fear not, for I am with you." After embracing Saint George, the Lord went back to heaven with His angels, in great glory.

In the morning, Saint George was brought before the tribune. He was singing a psalm saying, "Make haste O God to deliver me, make haste to help me O Lord." When he came to the tribune, he cried out saying, "O tribune, My Lord Jesus Christ and I have come to meet you and your stone god, Apollo." Dadianus tied him with four leather straps and beat him with leather whips upon his back and belly. He was thrown into prison.

Dadianus wrote a letter in which he said: "I write greetings to the whole world. Let any enchanter or magician who can put an end to the magic of this Christian, come to me now. I will give him much wealth and territory and I will make him second in my kingdom."

When this letter was sent throughout the world, a man named Athanasius came to the governor and said: "O king, live forever! There is nothing that I am not able to perform in your presence."

The governor rejoiced and said: "What sign will you work to put an end to the magic of this Christian called George?"

Athanasius answered and said: "Bring me an ox."

So the governor brought him an ox and Athanasius spoke certain words in the ears of the ox. The ox was split into two pieces and when weighed on scales, both parts weighed the same. Dadianus was convinced by the power of Athanasius. Saint George was brought into the tribune and Dadianus told him: "O George, it is for your sake that I have summoned this man into my dominion. You must vanquish his magic or he will vanquish you. You must kill him, or he will kill you."

Saint George looked at the magician and said: "Hasten my brother. Do to me as you wish to do."

Straightaway, Athanasius took a cup, washed his face in it and invoked the names of all the demons on it. He gave the cup to Saint George to drink, yet no evil befell him.

Athanasius answered and said to St George: "I will try one

more sign with you and if no evil befalls you, I will believe in the God whom they crucified."

Athanasius took another cup, washed his face in it and invoked the names of even stronger demons. Saint George drank the cup and no evil happened to him. When Athanasius saw this, he said: "O Saint George, you really do have the Cross of Jesus Christ, the Son of God, who came into the world to save sinners. Please have mercy on my soul and give me the seal of Christ."

When Dadianus saw what had happened, he was greatly enraged and he ordered that the magician be taken out of the city and slain with the sword. Thus, the magician consummated his martyrdom and was esteemed worthy of everlasting life. St George was thrown into prison as the governor thought of another means of torture.

When it was morning, the governor commanded that a huge wheel be made, with sharp nails and stakes fastened to it. The upper part of it was like the edge of a knife and the lower part like a sharp two-edged sword. When Saint George first saw the instrument, he said within himself: "Verily, I shall not come out of this instrument alive."

Then he said to himself again: "Woe to you George, how can you allow such a thought to enter your heart? Don't you remember how the Jews crucified Christ?"

Saint George lifted his eyes to heaven and said: "O Lord, the unchangeable God, the Ruler of eternity, to whom belong victory, I know that you give grace to your martyrs. You created the heavens and the earth. You rest upon the waters and the whole race of humanity. You spread out the heavens like a chamber and at your command, all clouds pour rain in due season. You rain upon the just and unjust. You weigh the mountains and hills and you bring winds out of store houses. You cast rebellious angels into the abyss of hell where they are punished by evil dragons and chained with indissoluble bonds. O Lord God, you sent your Only Begotten Son into this world and He took flesh through the Virgin Mary. You walked on the face of the sea and upon dry land. You fed five thousand men with five loaves of bread and they were satisfied. You rebuked the waves of the sea and they came down before you. Come now O my Lord. Come and help my infirmity, for I am a sinner. Let these sufferings be light upon me, for thine is the Glory and honour, forever, Amen."

As soon as he finished his prayer, he was thrown onto the wheel and immediately, his body was broken into ten pieces. Dadianus lifted his voice and said: "O governors, be strong and know that there is no god other than Apollo, Hermes, Zeus, Athene, Scamandros, Hephaistos, Herakles and Poseidon, who work good on the three parts of the sea and from whose hands kings receive power. Where is the God of Saint George whom they call Jesus and whom the Jews crucified and slew? Why has he not come and delivered him out of my hands?"

The bones of Saint George were thrown outside the city, in a dry pit so that other Christians do not take his bones and build a martyrium.

Now the seventy governors had gathered together to eat, when suddenly, the sky became overcast with clouds and a great earthquake occurred. The mountains split, the earth shook, the sea lashed into billows and the waves reached a height of fifteen cubits. Archangel Michael blew his trumpet and the Lord Jesus came upon a chariot of the Cherubim and stood at the edge of the pit. The Lord said to Archangel Michael, "Go down into the pit and gather the bones of my son George. This valiant son of mine, thought it would be impossible to survive the instrument, but now he will know that I alone are able to deliver him."

Archangel Michael went down into the pit and put together the holy body of Saint George. The Lord held the hand of Saint George and said: "O George my beloved, behold the hand which formed Adam, the first man, is now able to create you anew." The Lord breathed upon his face and filled him again with life. The Lord embraced him and went up to heaven with His holy angels.

Saint George arose from the dead in haste and went through the squares of the city, looking for the governors. He ran into their presence and told them: "Do you know who I am?"

Dadianus lifted his eyes guiltily and said: "Who are you?"

The saint said: "I am George whom you slew yesterday."

Dadianus looked at the saint's face deeply and said: "You are not George but you do look like him."

However, Anatolius, the General, realised that George had risen from the dead. Immediately, Anatolius and three thousand and ten other people believed in Christ. When Dadianus heard this, he ordered that all these believers be cast out of the city and slain. Thus, they were all martyred and received into eternal Glory.

The governor commanded soldiers to bring Saint George to the tribune and bind him to an iron bed. They melted lead until it was all liquid and thrust it into his mouth. They drove sixty nails into his head. Dadianus chiselled a great stone and fit it to his head. They rolled him down, with the stone, from a very high place. His bones were severed but he bore these tortures with fortitude. Dadianus hanged him upside down, tied another stone to him and lit a huge fire underneath him.

After these things, the governor commanded to throw Saint George into a bronze bull and to drive more sharp nails into him. The body of the saint was broken into pieces and his limbs became particles of dry summer dust. He was thrown into prison until the governor decided what to do with him next.

While in prison, the Lord appeared to St George saying, "Be patient O George, my chosen one, be of good cheer and do not be dismayed, for I am with you. There will be great Joy in heaven for your sake and for your contest. Behold, you have died once and I raised you up. You shall die another two times, but I will raise you up. On your fourth death, I will come to you on clouds and take you to the place of Joy, which I have prepared for you. I am the one who gives strength to your body. I will give you a place among Abraham, Isaac and Jacob. Do not be despondent for I am with you. Your martyrdom will be consummated before these seventy governors and you shall testify of Me before them. They will torture you for seven years, but be of good cheer."

The Lord saluted him and went up to heaven with His holy angels. Saint George rejoiced in the encouragement which the Lord had given him.

In the morning, the governor brought St George to the tribune again. When he was brought in, one of the seventy governors, whose name was Magnentius, said to him: "O George, I seek a sign from you. If you fulfil this sign, I will believe in your God and worship Him nobly."

So Saint George said to him, "What sign do you ask of me?"

Magnentius, the governor, said to him: "There are seventy thrones here, a throne for each governor here. The legs of each throne is made of various kinds of wood, some fruit bearing and some not. Now, if you pray and make each wooden leg take root and blossom with fruit and leaves, I will believe in your God."

Saint George threw himself upon his face and prayed for a long time. After he finished his prayer, he said "Amen" and rose up. Immediately, there was trembling and shaking, for the Spirit of God came upon the thrones and they budded and blossomed and brought forth fruit. Then Magnentius the governor, said to him, "A great god is Herakles who has manifested his power in dry wood."

Saint George answered and said: "Will you compare this blind and dumb idol Herakles with the God who made the heavens and the earth?"

Dadianus the governor, answered and saint to Saint George, "O excellent Galilean, I know how I will destroy you."

Dadianus commanded the soldiers to bring a huge saw and they cut Saint George into two pieces. The saint yielded up his spirit. His body was put into a large cauldron of lead, pitch, animal fat and bitumen. They boiled these contents until the flames went up to a great height. After this, the soldiers brought pieces from the cauldron to the king, saying: "This (wretched man) has come to an end and is burnt up." Dadianus commanded them to bury the cauldron and the pieces of the saint which were in it, into the earth, lest the Christians find his body and build a martyrium.

When the attendants had buried the saint, there was great trembling in the air so that the earth shook. The Lord Jesus came down from heaven with His holy angels, stood over the place where the cauldron was buried and said to Zalathiel, the angel: "Bring out the cauldron."

The Lord then said: "O George, my chosen one, Arise! I raised Lazareth from the dead and I command you to arise and come out of the cauldron. I am the Lord, your God."

Straightaway, Saint George rose with great power as one who had suffered no pain at all. Everyone who saw the saint, marvelled.

The Lord said to the saint: "Be strong and of good cheer, George, my beloved, for there will be great Joy over you, in heaven and on earth. Be strong for I am with you." The Lord Jesus then went up to heaven, with His holy angels.

Saint George arose and sent to the governor saying: "I am going around the city, teaching." Immediately, the governor commanded the soldiers to seize the saint and return him to the tribune. Saint George walked to the tribune, saying: "O tribune, O tribune, My Lord Jesus Christ and I are coming to you and to your god Apollo."

On the way, a woman whose name was Schollastike, cried out to Saint George saying: "O George, my son was yoking his ox in the field, when the ox fell down and died. Please help me because I know you are able to do anything through your God."

Saint George said to her: "Take this staff and lay it on the dead ox while saying: "In the name of Jesus, arise and stand up.""

The woman did as she was told and the ox rose from the dead straightaway.

The woman glorified God saying: "Blessed is the hour in which George came into the city. Surely he is a prophet and God has visited his people."

Trakiali, the governor, spoke to George saying: "Concerning the dry wood that budded, we do not know if it was your God, or our god. So I want you to perform one more sign. We have a sepulchre cut in the rock on the road to the cemetery, but no one knows where it is. I want you to pray so that the bones of those buried within, may arise. Then, I promise you, I will believe in your God and become a Christian."

The blessed Saint George answered and said: "If you have faith as a mustard seed, you shall say to this mountain "Move" and it shall move from there as nothing is impossible. Therefore, arise, open the door of the tomb and bring to me the rotten bones of those who were dead, together with their dust."

Three governors went to the place of the sepulchre and opened the door, but they found no bones at all, so they took the bone dust which they found, and brought it to Saint George. Saint George threw himself on his knees and prayed. As soon as he finished his prayer, the earth trembled and flashes of light shone upon the bones. Five men, nine woman and three children were brought forth. When the governors saw this, they marvelled.

The governor cried out to one of those who had risen from the dead, saying, "What is your name?"

He that had risen from the dead, said: "My name is Boes."

Dadianus said to him: "How many years have you been dead for?"

The man replied: "For more than two hundred years."

Dadianus asked: "Had Christ come into the world at that time or not?"

The man replied: "I do not know, neither did I hear that He had come."

So Dadianus said to him: "Which god do you believe in?"

The dead man answered: "O governor, do not force me for I am ashamed to say which god I believe in. I believed in Apollo, a stupid, dumb, deaf and blind idol. When I died, I was taken to a river of fire and to a place of worms. There is no mercy there and the Judge is not persuaded. Every man's work is laid before his eyes. Every person who lived on earth and confessed Him who they crucified, was given rest on the Lord's day. But as for me, I was not given rest because I did not confess Christ when I was on earth. Why do you worship idols and images that cannot move?"

Dadianus answered: "Your senses have been destroyed over these two hundred years."

The man who had risen from the dead, looked at Saint George and said to him: "O martyr of Christ, we beseech you to give us the Holy Baptism of Christ, so that we may not go back to the punishment of where we were."

When Saint George saw their faith, he smote the earth with his foot, water welled up and he baptised them in the name of the Father, the Son and the Holy Spirit. Saint George told them: "Depart in peace to Paradise" and immediately they disappeared.

Dadianus was stupefied. The governors who were with him, said, "This man is a magician, and by his magic, he makes demons rise up before us."

Dadianus said: "I will now disgrace the whole race of Christians."

He commanded that the poorest widow be brought to him. He took Saint George to the widow's house, so as to disgrace the reputation of all Christians. Saint George told the widow: "Give me some bread for I am hungry."

The widow answered: "Master, I have no bread in my house."

Saint George said to her: "Which god do you believe in?"

The woman said: "I believe in Apollo and Herakles, the almighty imperial gods."

Saint George said to her: "Truly, it is a just judgement from God, that you have no bread in the house."

When the woman saw that the face of Saint George was like that of an angel, she said within herself: "I will go and beg bread from my neighbours that I may set it before this man of God."

As soon as the widow left the house, Saint George sat by the foot of the wooden pillar in her house and it immediately brought root and leaves. It became a large tree and towered up fifteen cubits, above the house. Michael, the archangel, came to Saint George with a table filled with good things. The saint ate and was comforted and left the rest for the widow. When the widow returned and saw these great marvels, she said within herself: "The God of the Christians has remembered my poverty and has brought this martyr to my house to help my wretched spirit." Immediately, she threw herself down, at the feet of the saint, and worshipped him. Saint George answered and said to her: "Rise up and stand on your feet for I am not the God of the Christians. I am only His servant."

The widow said to him: "Master, if I have found favour before you, allow me to say one thing."

So Saint George said: "Speak."

The woman said: "Master, I have a little boy who is nine years old. He is blind, deaf, dumb and lame and I am ashamed to show him to my neighbours. If you heal him, I will believe in your God."

Saint George said: "Bring the child to me."

The widow brought her child from the third storey of the house and laid him in the bosom of the righteous man. Saint George prayed over him, with his head bowed down, over the child. The saint breathed on him and scales fell from his eyes, and the child was able to see.

The woman cried out: "Master, I beg you, make him speak and hear and stand on his feet."

But Saint George told her: "O woman, this is sufficient for now. When I need him, I will call him and he shall hear me and come and serve with me."

The widow was not able to utter a single word because she saw that the saint's face was like the face of the angel of God.

As Dadianus and the sixty-nine other governors, were

walking through the city, they saw the tree which had sprung out of the poor widow's house.

Dadianus said: "What is this new fig tree?"

The other governors told him: "This is the place into which George, the mighty saint of the Galileans, was cast."

Immediately, Dadianus brought George to the public assembly where he was flogged without mercy. His flesh was cut into pieces and his body was placed alight, and consumed by the flame. Saint George was hanged over iron pots of fire. The saint yielded up his spirit.

Dadianus cast the saint's body over a high mountain, called Siris, in the hope that birds would come and devour his flesh. Immediately, there came mighty thunders and lightings so that the whole mountain shook. The Lord appeared on a cloud and said to Saint George, "O excellent and chosen one, rise up." Immediately, the saint arose. He ran after the attendants and said: "Wait for me, I am coming with you." When the attendants saw this, they glorified God and threw themselves at the feet of the saint, saying: "Give us the seal of Christ." Saint George baptised them, and they came and stood before the lawless governor and shouted: "We are CHRISTIANS." The governors were speechless.

Dadianus took Klaudane, one of the attendants, and crucified him. He took Lasiri and Lasiriane, another two attendants, and killed them with the sword. The last attendant, Klekon, was thrown to wild beasts.

After this, Saint George was brought before the governor again. Dadianus told him, "O George, I swear by all my gods, that I will treat you kindly, as a beloved son. I will give you everything you ask for if only you will worship my gods."

Saint George said to him: "I marvel at your words. I have been wanting power for a long time. Why didn't you tell me this before? You have tortured me for the past seven years, I died three times, I rose three times, but I have never heard you say these things. I rejoice because I want power. I will therefore, sacrifice to your god Apollo, whom you love."

When Dadianus, the governor, heard these things, he rejoiced greatly, took hold of the hand of Saint George and kissed it.

Saint George resisted him, saying: "No, governor, it is not a custom of the Galileans to be treated like this unless they have first worshipped to the gods. Command that I be put in prison until tomorrow."

The governor answered: "Forgive me for all the sufferings I have inflicted on you, for I did it all in ignorance. Accept me now as a father and I will take you into my palace to where Queen Alexandria is resting."

The governor brought the saint into the Queen's chamber and locked them both in the room. Saint George bowed his knees and prayed saying: "O God, my God, there is none like you for you do marvellous things. Why do the heathen cry out and the why do people believe in vain gods? All the governors and rulers of this earth speak against you, O God."

Queen Alexandria heard his prayer and said: "O George, my master, I am listening attentively to you words and I like them. Who are these who cry out? Who are these vain gods? Who is Christ? Teach me."

Saint George answered and said: "If you desire to know Christ, then listen to what I will say. After God created heaven and earth, he took some dust from the earth and made man in His image. Thus, He made flesh out of earth. This means, we are all made of dust. The Lord Himself took flesh from the Holy Virgin Saint Mary and became man. He is the God who raised me up from the dead, and it is for HIS sake that I am enduring all these sufferings. It is my God who created the heavens, the sun, the shining moon, the stars and all creation."

The Queen answered him: "Explain these matters to me."

So Saint George said to her: "The idolaters who are in the world today, worship abominable things and not God. They serve soul-less idols, fashioned by the hands of man. They despise God, the real creator of this universe."

The Queen said to him: "Then are these vain gods like demons?"

Saint George said to her: "Yes, they are demons."

So the Queen said: "How did the Son of God come into the world?"

Saint George answered her saying: "O Queen Alexandra, listen to me. David, the prophet, said that God sits upon the Cherubim, and will come down to help us. He shall come down as rain upon mown grass, which refers to the Virgin Saint Mary. Similarly, Habakkuk, the prophet heard the voice of God and remained speechless. Habakkuk prophesised that Jesus would come down into this world to deliver us from the snares of the devil. The devil is the one who has stolen the truth from our seventy governors."

The Queen answered saying: "Truly, you have convinced

me that your God is the God of the universe. Please pray for me so that God may deliver me from all the wiles of the devil."

St George told her: "If you believe in the Lord Jesus and in the power of His cross, no demon shall draw near you at all."

The Queen replied: "I believe but I am afraid of Dadianus because he is so wicked. He devours flesh like a wild beast. Please keep this matter secret and tell no one."

The next morning, the herald sounded: "All people are to gather together to see Saint George worship Apollo." The whole city was gathered to see the sight.

The saint was brought into the courtyard of the temple where he was to offer sacrifices. Saint George told the attendants: "You can go back to the governor, while the priests and I will go to Apollo and worship him."

When the poor widow, whose son Saint George had cured, heard this, she uncovered her hair, rent her clothes and set out to see the saint.

When she saw the saint, the widow cried out: "Why are you going to Apollo and disgracing the race of Christians? With your God, you raised the dead, you made the blind to see, you made pieces of wood to blossom, you made the pillar of my house to root, you filled my table with bread and good things. You performed so many miracles and put the devil to shame. What are you doing now?"

When Saint George heard this, he smiled to the widow and called for her son. Saint George said to the little child: "In the name of my Lord Jesus Christ, I want you to be my servant in this matter. I want you to go to the idol of Apollo and say, "George, the servant of Christ, calls for you.""

The young child leapt in Joy and did as he was told.

He went to Apollo and said: "O blind, dumb and senseless idol, come forth quickly for Saint George calls for you."

Immediately, the evil spirit in the idol cried out: "O Nazarene, will you draw everyone to you? You even sent me this young boy to disgrace me."

Straightaway, the idol of Apollo leapt down from its pedestal and came to Saint George.

The saint asked him: "Are you the god of the heathen?"

The demon in the idol said: "Bear with me a little and I will explain myself."

Saint George said: "Speak."

So the demon began to open up and say: "You know that God created Man in His own image and placed him in the garden of Eden. God called for all the angels to come and worship him so Michael and his army of angels obeyed. However, I could not worship a man whom God had created. I disputed the command of God because I knew that I was better than Man. Immediately, God cast me from heaven, I lost all my glory and came into this idol. Now I lead away the children of Man."

As soon as Saint George heard the story, he said: "O demon, you speak lies. You were cast from heaven on account of your pride. You prepared a throne for yourself and made yourself equal to God."

When the demon heard these things, he was speechless. Saint George smote the earth with his foot, and the earth opened up.

The saint said: "Go down into the abyss, O unclean spirit. Give speech to all the souls you have destroyed."

The unclean spirit fell into the earth with the idol in which it had dwelt. Again, the saint smote the earth with his foot and the earth closed back.

Saint George went to the idol of Herakles, pulled it to the ground and broke it to pieces. The saint said: "You too, go down into the abyss for I have come against you in anger and wrath."

When the priests and the ministers saw the destruction that had been caused, they tied Saint George and brought him to the governor. When Dadianus heard that his idols had been thrown into the abyss, he was filled with fury.

He said to Saint George: "You deserve all destruction! Didn't you tell me that you will worship my gods? Didn't you say you would throw incense to them? Why do you work magic like that? Your life is in my hands and I can kill you."

So Saint George said: "Go and bring Apollo to me and I will worship him before you."

Dadianus said: "I was just told that you sent Apollo into the abyss."

Saint George said: "If Apollo was the mighty god, how come he could not help himself?"

Dadianus was greatly grieved so he went to meet Queen Alexandra.

He told her: "I am sick of these Christians, in particular the Galilean, George."

Queen Alexandra answered him saying, "How many

times have I told you to leave George? His God is the true God and He can destroy you."

The governor answered: "Woe to you Alexandra. I think the magic of these Christians has entered into you." Immediately, Dadianus dragged Queen Alexandra from her hair and brought her to the sixty-nine governors. She was hanged onto a wooded horse and tortured, yet she did not speak a word. When Queen Alexandra saw Saint George, she cried out: "Pray for me while I suffer these tortures."

Saint George answered her: "Bear them patiently, O Queen, so that you can receive crowns of martyrdom."

The Queen replied: "But what should I do for I have not been baptised."

The saint assured her: "The pouring of your holy blood is a baptism."

Queen Alexandra then lifted up a prayer saying: "O my Lord Jesus Christ, I have kept the door of my palace open before you. Please do not close the door of Paradise before me."

After having said this, the Queen consummated her martyrdom and received her incorruptible crown.

After seeing these things, Dadianus said to Saint George, "Behold, you have destroyed the Queen, and now I will gain mastery over you."

Magnentius, one of the governors, said: "Let us sentence him to death."

So Dadianus wrote his sentence of death, saying: "I give George, the chief of Galileans, over to the sword. George has disobeyed the decree of sixty-nine governors so we are innocent of his blood this day."

The saint was then brought to the site of martyrdom. The saint looked up to the soldiers who were holding him and said: "Brethren, bear with me a little while I pray for the seventy governors who have tortured me for the past seven years."

The saint looked up to heaven and said: "O my Lord Jesus Christ, you listened to Elijah and sent fire from heaven to devour the two captains of fifty and their hundred soldiers. Please, bring down the same fire and devour the seventy governors and those standing with them, for to You is all Glory and Power."

Immediately, a fire fell from heaven and devoured the seventy governors with their hosts. Five thousand people died that day.

The Saint continued praying: "My Lord Jesus Christ, allow my name to heal all those afflicted by unclean spirits. Have mercy on all those who remember my name. Write the names of all the people who document my sufferings in your Book of Life. If the heavens withhold their rain, and people call upon me, answer them speedily, O Lord. Remember all those who show kindness to the poor, on my name. O Lord, Jesus Christ, I have suffered all these pains for the sake of Your name."

After the saint had said these things, the Lord Jesus Christ appeared to him, saying: "Come up to heaven with me. I have prepared for you a place in the Kingdom of my Father. O George, I will fulfil everything that you have asked for, and many other things, greater than these."

Saint George stretched out his neck and said to the executioners: "Come now and perform what has been commanded of you." The saint was beheaded and water and milk flowed forth. Jesus Christ took his blessed soul, embraced it and took it up to heaven with him. He offered it as a gift to His Good Father and the Holy Spirit. Immediately, the earth shook and there was mighty thunder and lightning.

All those who had become martyrs with Saint George were eight thousand, six hundred and ninety-nine, together with Alexandra the Queen.

I, Pasikrates, the servant of Saint George, have been with the saint throughout his entire contest. I have written down his martyrdom and have not added or taken away anything. The Lord Jesus Christ helped me, to Him be all the Glory and Honour, Amen.

THE ENCOMIUM BY SAINT THEODOSIUS

The Lord performed many miracles on the hands of Saint George.

Miracles were reported after his martyrdom and after his body was brought to Diospolis, his native city. Miracles were also performed after the building of his shrine, which was completed and consecrated on the seventh of Hatour. Saint Theodosius, Bishop of Jerusalem, recites many of these miracles.

> "I will open my mouth in parables. I will declare the things which have been hidden from the beginning, which we have heard and known, and which our fathers have declared unto us."

As the Holy Spirit spoke on the mouth of David, the

righteous king, so also, I will tell of miracles that have been performed through St George, the mighty martyr of Christ.

Tyre was the city of King Nebuchadnezzar, king of the Chaldeans. This king forsook Tyre and went to Babylon where he built and fortified the city in a royal manner. After the head of Saint George was cut off during his martyrdom, it was said that his head had totally separated from his body from the ninth hour of the day. Pasikrates, the servant of St George, stood by the body, weeping and watching over it. Several people from the city also came to see the body, after they heard of the death of Saint George. When they put the head of the saint back onto his body, the head joined again as if nothing had happened to it. They brought a napkin to smear the blood on his body. The saint was wrapped in cloth and laid in a new sepulchre, near the outside of the city. The following day, they brought incense and linen to lay on his body. Again they saw that the head had been united to the body and the sword stroke was not even present. The servants marvelled greatly and believed in the God of Saint George. The sepulchre was sealed and Pasikrates stood outside to watch. Two servants went back into the city to work and save money for the return of the saint's body back to his country. After having worked for two months, the Lord sent a merchant ship from Joppa where the sailors agreed to ship the body of the saint for a certain price of money. When the sailors heard that it was the body of Saint George, they marvelled greatly, after hearing the manner of his martyrdom. They rose and worshipped God who esteemed them worthy of carrying the saint in their ship. One of the sailors, Leontius, who was an acquaintance of Saint George, brought horses, laid the saint's body on them and carried it to his house at Diospolis.

By that time, Saint George's mother and sisters had gone to rest. Report spread abroad that the body of Saint George had returned home, after an absence of seven years. When the Christians reached the house, they wept, worshipped and marvelled at the things which had taken place. Pasikrates and two other servants, Lukios and Kirinneos, told the people of the city everything that Saint George had endured. Again, the people marvelled and rejoiced that they were worthy of receiving such a saint. The body of the saint was laid at his home for a week where everyone came and worshipped it. On the day of the festival, everyone assembled in the church and the story of Saint George's martyrdom was read to all the believers. There was a wealthy nobleman called Andrew, of the family of Saint George's mother. He was touched by the story read especially the promises that God told Saint George: "He who confesses your sufferings will not be subject to harm. He who remembers your name will not fear judgement or any affliction. He who writes of your martyrdom will have their name written in the Book of Life. He who offers charity in your name will be numbered amongst the saints. I am the Lord God and that which I have done, I will do. I will never forsake him who builds a shrine on your name. I will perform miracles wherever your body is laid. I will make all nations come to your shrine and bring gifts. Everyone shall gather at your shrine, Jews, Samaritans, Persians, the children of Esau and even the barbarians."

When Andrew heard these promises, he was filled with Joy and immediately rose up and wrote the martyrdom of Saint George and put it in his house, saying: "I will set the memorial of my brother in my house, that his blessing and favour may abide with me forever."

Andrew then cried out amongst all the people: "My brethren, let us now rejoice for our brother has received great honour in heaven. He has received freedom of speech before God and is able to entreat God on our behalf so that we may receive mercy in this world and in what is to come. Now my brethren, let us build a shrine on his name and lay his body in it, that his blessing and favour may abide in us forever."

All the people answered in one voice, "Let it all be done. If you undertake this matter, we will undertake it with you, that the blessing of the saint may be with us and our children."

Hearing this, Andrew rejoiced. He rose up early the next morning and called servants and labourers. He pulled down the dwelling house of the saint and said: "I will not lay my brother's body in strange ground."

The body of the saint was taken to the church while all the labourers cleared down the saint's old house and built new foundations for a shrine.

THE MIRACLES OF SAINT GEORGE

FIRST MIRACLE

The first miracle performed on the name of Saint George, occurred in the building of the shrine where the saint's body was to be lain. It came to pass that Andrew was lying in his bed one night and thinking within himself: "No man is willing to help me in building this shrine and I am not sure if I can finish it on my own. If I do not finish it, men will laugh at me because I began to build but was unable to finish." While he was meditating on these things, he unintentionally slept. Saint George appeared to him in a dream saying, "Andrew, Andrew, do you know me?"

When Andrew recognised that it was Saint George, he was astonished and said: "Are you alive, O George, my master?"

Saint George replied: "Thanks be to God, my body is with you, but I live with God by the Holy Spirit. I see that you are downhearted about the shrine which you have started to build in my name. I have come to show you some wealth which belongs to my ancestors, out of which you may pay for the shrine. Be of good cheer and do not be faint hearted, for I will put it in the hearts of people, to come and help you. Now arise and follow me for I want to show you the room in my house in which my body was laid."

So Andrew, in his dream, rose up and followed the saint. Saint George took him to the room where he was lain and placed a mark with his finger saying, "Rise up early in the morning and come here. Dig down one cubit and you will find a blessing which God has set apart for you."

When Andrew woke from his vision, he roused his wife and told her everything that he had seen. Both marvelled greatly.

His wife said to him: "Let us rise up now, light a lamp and go to the place which Saint George has told you about. If we see the mark that Saint George has put with his finger, then surely the vision you saw was true."

So both set out to the place which the saint had directed them to. They arrived to the place at midnight, with Andrew carrying a spade and his wife carrying the lamp. They saw the mark which Saint George had made with his finger and this proved to them that Saint George really had appeared in the vision. Andrew started digging and when he had gone down a little way, he found a jar having its mouth sealed with clay. They both fell on the ground, worshipping God. They went back home, opened the jar to find it filled with gold. Andrew took out two hins of gold wherewith he may complete the building of the shrine. He buried the remainder in his house, keeping it well hidden.

In the morning, Andrew wished to make a feast for all the city, in the name of Saint George because he wanted to give his first fruits to the Lord. He invited all the poor, infirm, widows and orphans in the city and ministered to them. The next day, he invited the nobles of the city and made another great feast for them in the name of Saint George. While they were eating, Andrew arose and said: "Since God has put it into your hearts, may everyone give a little of what he has so that we may build a great martyrium for Saint George. Our generation will be blessed for we have the honour of receiving the body of such great a saint."

The nobles answered him in one voice, "We will act according to our power."

Surely, two thousand pounds in gold and one thousand silver were gathered for the shrine of Saint George.

After this, the shrine was built and completed in three years. The body of the holy martyr was brought into the martyrium and the Bishop of Jerusalem consecrated the shrine. Many miracles occurred at the shrine. Many people were cured and a multitude of unclean spirits had come out through the name of Saint George.

SECOND MIRACLE

When the holy Bishop had consecrated the shrine of Saint George, a man with an unclean spirit came in. This evil spirit used to bring him to the ground, inflict suffering on him and make him foam at the mouth. The man stood amongst the congregation, hoping to be blessed. When the Bishop started bringing up the holy offering, the evil spirit pushed the man onto the ground and he started foaming at the mouth again. He then rose up and cried: "What have you to do with me, O saint of God? I know who you are and you will not be able to cast me out of this man for you have no authority over me." The evil spirit continued to blaspheme against God and Saint George.

Saint George tied the inflicted man to a pillar so that his hands were tied back to the pillar without any rope, and his feet did not touch the ground. The Saint held the body of the inflicted man in this position. When people saw this, they marvelled. The saint let go of the man and he fell to the ground as though having died. Suddenly, a lame man walked into the shrine. The man who had been demon possessed took hold of the neck of the lame man. Immediately, the legs of the lame man gave a crack and straightened. The lame man gained strength and was healed.

The demon possessed man then walked to the Bishop and said: "Forgive me, O holy father, and I will tell you what I have seen. I have been possessed by the devil all my life, but today I saw Saint George and am healed. When I first saw the saint, I was frightened but then Saint George came to me from the altar, took hold of my hand and comforted me. He inflicted great sufferings on the devil inside me and made it depart. Saint George lifted the demon to the top of the pillar and threw him onto the pavement. The devil vowed never to enter me again. I was relieved. Then I saw this lame man walk inside the shrine. Saint George held my hands and placed them on the neck of this lame man. He told me to hold onto the neck tightly. As I held his neck, I saw Saint George hold the legs of this lame man. Immediately, the man arose and went away running. Saint George then went back to heaven."

When the Bishop and the multitudes heard this story,

they marvelled greatly and glorified God saying: "Great are the mighty deeds and favours which God works through His saints."

This man, who was once demon possessed, became a full-time servant in the shrine of Saint George. He served there day and night until his death.

THIRD MIRACLE

There was a certain Jew who was a sorcerer and a thief. He would put people to sleep through his sorcery and then steal their possessions. He heard about the miracles performed through Saint George, but he did not believe them. He would blaspheme against Saint George in front of many multitudes and say: "The Christians are mistaken. They pray to this earthly human and ask him to heal their diseases."

When a certain feeble-hearted Christian heard these blasphemies, he said: "God will not allow you to continue with these blasphemies. The saint will defend himself and seek revenge against you."

So the Jew answered: "I will go into the shrine of Saint George, plunder it, steal all its possessions and let us see what the saint will do to me."

So the Christian said, "Let us vow three pounds of gold. If some evil befalls you because of your evil act, you will pay me three pounds of gold and become Christian. However, if nothing occurs, I will pay you the three pounds of gold."

Then the Jew, who was also a sorcerer, went into the shrine and stole some possessions without anyone realising. As he walked out the door of the shrine, he said within himself, "Be ashamed now Saint George. Be ashamed O man who vowed three pounds of gold. I will surely make this man forsake his faith and deny his baptism. I will see what this dead Saint George will do."

As the Jew was thinking within himself, Saint George appeared to him in the form of a soldier. He was holding a large ox-hide leather whip and he spoke to the Jew, saying: "My brother, what are you carrying? Show me."

The Jew was astonished and said: "Friend, I will hide nothing from you. I have stolen a few things and since God has led you to me, I will give you a portion of these things. However, you must not tell any man."

Saint George replied: "I accept. Let us go into the shrine and divide these things between us."

As they entered the shrine, Saint George gave him a blow on the head with the whip, saying, "Do you know who I am?"

The Jew said: "No, I do not know you."

The saint said to him: "I am George."

As soon as the Jew heard this, he trembled and fell onto the ground. The Saint took hold of him and dragged him saying: "Come with me and I will tell you who I really am."

The Saint bound him in the shrine, tied the things which he had stolen and began to lash him with the whip he held in his hand. The Jew cried aloud and the multitude looked back to see what was happening.

The people started asking themselves, "Who has suspended this man?"

Immediately, the Jew confessed what he had done.

The people marvelled at what had happened.

When they went to grab a ladder and untie him, the steward said: "Let him who suspended him, bring him down."

The Jew was left tied until the morning. He began to cry

and say: "O George, my master, have mercy on me and I will never steal again. I will become a Christian and I will never practise sorcery again."

When Saint George saw the fixedness of his intentions, he had compassion on him, came by the night and brought him down. Immediately, the Jew returned everything that he had stolen. He wrote a letter to his wife and relatives in Jerusalem and told them what had happened. When his relatives read the letter, they marvelled at the amazing wonders of Saint George. When the Christian who had vowed three pounds of gold, heard the story, he began to marvel too. The Jew was baptised in the shrine of Saint George and became a Christian. His family, relatives and a great multitude of Jews were also baptised that day.

FOURTH MIRACLE

The miracles of Saint George grew widespread and all the people of the city heard of them. There was a certain man from Persia, called Nicanor. He ruled over a third of Persia and had a leprous son called Anatolius. When he heard of the miracles of Saint George, he cried saying, "If God performs a miracle through the prayers of Saint George, I will dedicate one hundred pounds of gold to the shrine of the saint and my whole household will become Christian."

The following day, his son was healed of his leprosy. When Nicanor, the ruler of the Persians, saw this great miracle, he rose up, took the gifts he had vowed and embarked in ships to the shrine of Saint George. He washed his healed son in the bath and anointed him with oil from the lamp. The son was baptised and all the multitudes glorified God.

When Nicanor returned to his land, he built a large church and dedicated it to Saint George. A Bishop was called from Antioch to consecrate the church. A multitude of Persians were baptised that day.

FIFTH MIRACLE

There were two Samaritans (partners in business) who wanted to buy one hundred pounds worth of merchandise. They saddled their donkeys and journeyed to Damascus to buy the merchandise. During their journey, they were talking about the miracles of Saint George. The night fell upon them and two hungry and roaring lions came out of the woods and stood before them on the road. When the donkeys saw the lions, they ran away terror-stricken. The men fell from their donkeys, half dead with fright. Immediately, one of the men said: "If Saint George delivers us from the mouths of these lions, we will send these hundred pounds of gold to the shrine of the saint and we will become Christian."

After they made this vow, God tamed the lions as he had done with Daniel the prophet. The lions bowed their heads downwards and returned to the woods. The men knew it was

Saint George who had protected them so they glorified God. After continuing on their journey, they found their donkeys grazing and unharmed. They rode on them again and reached their town safely. Everyone in the town heard of the amazing miracle and glorified God. The men of the city said: "These wild beasts have destroyed several men, but glory be to God who has delivered you from this wrath."

The men continued into Damascus, brought some merchandise in order to sell and make profit. The profit was vowed to Saint George. They found some precious diamonds which they bought for one hundred pounds and sold them for two hundred pounds of gold. They took the profit to the shrine of Saint George and were baptised. One hundred and fifty-three souls became Christian that day in the shrine of the saint.

SIXTH MIRACLE

There was a certain Christian in Jerusalem whose name was Zograter. The man was rich, with much gold, silver and herds of cattle, however, he could not walk on his feet and his son was a lunatic. When he heard about the miracles of Saint George, he vowed saying, "If Saint George heals my feet and legs, I will send three meals and three pints of wine to his shrine every month. If the saint heals me before his feast day, I will WALK to his shrine and offer one hundred pounds of gold too."

After making this vow, his legs became smaller, his body loosened and he was able to walk freely again. He walked to his nearby church and prayed: "I thank you God of Saint George for you healed my body within two days."

On the feast day of Saint George, his servants asked him:

"Which animal shall we prepare for the ride?" However, Zograter answered and said: "As the Lord lives, I will walk on my legs from Jerusalem to the shrine of Saint George for I have made a vow."

When he arrived at the shrine, multitudes of people began to glorify God after hearing the miracle. Zograter offered his gifts, just as he had promised.

When the steward saw the great gifts which Zograter was offering, he took him to his house and accommodated him for two months. On the third day, Zograter's son arose to see what had happened to his father for he had not yet returned from the shrine.

Now Zograter was talking to the steward and saying: "My son is possessed by a devil and he is continually tormented. If Saint George heals my son, I will bring greater gifts to his shrine."

The steward said to him, "Do you believe that God is able to do everything?"

Zograter answered: "I believe that nothing is too hard for Him."

As they were talking, Zograptor's son came riding to the shrine, accompanied with several servants. They enquired about Zograptor and found him with the steward. When Zograptor's son entered the shrine, the devil inflicted him greatly and he began to foam at the mouth and say: "What are you doing to me George? Why do you trouble me so much? I am a lunatic and no one will cast me out." The devil continued to speak blasphemies but Saint George smote him with severe smitings. Again, the devil cried out, "O George, you make me suffer." Immediately, the devil came out of Zograptor's son and he was healed. When Zograptor saw this, he glorified God and offered many gifts to the shrine of the saint. Every year, on the feast of Saint George, Zograptor would come to the shrine of the saint and invite all the widows and orphans for a feast.

SEVENTH MIRACLE

The servants of the shrine of Saint George began to increase. The stewards made them go out and collect all the gifts which were offered to the shrine. Many barren women had bore children through the intercessions of Saint George so many children were dedicated and vowed to the shrine too. When a storm broke out at sea, the sailors would cry to Saint George and he would bring them safely to their haven. Many sailors would then vow cattle to the shrine of the saint. One of the servants in the shrine used to steal this property and take it to their house. Saint George bore with him for five years, in the hope that he would repent, however, he continued in his evil way. Saint George then inflicted a wicked devil into him, who tormented him day and night. The servant suffered for two months. After this, he ran to the church and confessed his thefts. Saint George had compassion on him and healed him. Multitudes of people glorified God.

EIGHTH MIRACLE

There was a rich man in Antioch, called Eulogios. He was occupied in great business and he owned a ship which went out to sea. He gave great charities to the poor, and many gifts and first fruits to the churches of Antioch. Twice a year, he prepared a feast for all the clergy of the city and he ate and drank frequently with the Archbishop. He prayed often and visited prisoners. On the feast of Saint George, he would visit the shrine, offer money and eat with the steward. He continued doing these good deeds for twelve years. However, the devil was envious of him. Eulogios owned a ship and it was tied to the shore. One night, the sky began to cloud with darkness and a great storm arose. The wind carried the ship away and no one knew where it had gone. Eulogios and his wife were very sorrowful, yet they thanked God and yielded to His will. However, the devil fought them with a greater trial than this. There was a very skilful Egyptian thief. By Satan's luck, he found a ship which took him to Antioch and directed him to Eulogios' house. He accommodated with Eulogios for a few days and became his labourer for two years. Eulogios trusted him and did not know that he was a thief. The thief spent a lot of time with Eulogios so he knew everything in the house.

The thief conspired with another two companions to rob the house of Eulogios. On the feast of Saint George, Eulogios and a group of people went to the shrine of the saint. While they were there, the mother-in-law of Eulogios fell sick and died. Eulogios' wife went to weep for her, leaving the house to the Egyptian thief. The thief called his two companions and they robbed the entire house, taking all the gold and silver. They took these possessions onto a ship and journeyed to Alexandria. They sold these treasures and earned three thousand pounds in gold. When Eulogios returned from the shrine and found out about his stolen house, he grieved greatly, yet again, he yielded to the will of God.

Meanwhile, those who had stolen his property, went to Peremoun and lived there. One of them fell sick and got possessed by a devil so he travelled away. A few days later, a quarrel arose between the other two so that the Egyptian rose at midnight and slew his second companion. He took all the gold and went to Palestine where he toiled in business.

Despite the trials they had suffered, Eulogios and his wife continued to offer gifts and alms to the shrine of Saint George. They continued giving their first fruits to the church and they continued serving the poor. However, the feast of Saint George came again but this time they had nothing to offer because they had been stolen.

Eulogios cried out: "Behold, all the people of the city are going to the shrine of Saint George, but we have no income this year to give. O Saint George, please look upon our affliction."

Eulogios' wife answered: "I know that we have nothing to give but I still have two garments. Take this good garment and sell it for money, so that our offerings to the shrine may not cease."

When Eulogios heard these things, his eyes filled with tears and they both wept.

The wife then said: "Look, rise up and go to our neighbours. I am sure they will have compassion and lend us some money so that you can go to the shrine in peace. If they do not lend us money, then sell this garment and may God's will be done."

Eulogios went to his neighbour and said: "The feast of Saint George is coming up, yet I do not have any money because of all the trials which have happened to me this year. I really want to offer something at the shrine so can you please lend me some money, which I can pay you later?"

While Eulogios was speaking, his neighbour's eyes filled with tears and he said to him, "My brother, I have three pounds of gold. Take them and if you need more, I will give you, so that I may obtain the blessings of the martyr too."

Eulogios and his wife rejoiced exceedingly and set off to the shrine of the saint.

Meanwhile, the Egyptian thief, who had stolen from the property of Eulogios, meditated within himself, saying: "I have sinned from my youth. I will suffer everlasting condemnation because I slew my companion and because I have stolen many things. I must go to the shrine of the saint and plead for mercy."

Behold, as the Egyptian thief entered into the shrine of Saint George, Eulogios saw him and noticed that he was wearing a robe that once belonged to him. Immediately, Eulogios bound him and took him to the steward because he was the one who had stolen his property. The steward asked the thief, "What have you done with the things you have stolen?"

The thief answered, "I have stolen nothing. O my master Eulogios, you know that I served you for two years and that I have never stolen anything from you. I bought this robe from the market. I know, it looks like yours."

The steward said to him, "I will only believe you if you go to the altar of Saint George and swear that you have not stolen."

The thief was glad that he was going to escape so he cried saying, "I will swear in whatever way you please."

The steward took him to the altar to make his oath.

Meanwhile, Saint George came to the steward in a vision and said: "This man has stolen. Do not let him go until you punish him and until he returns everything back."

The steward brought two new whips and beat the Egyptian thief. He told the thief: "You either return all the stolen possessions or you will be whipped to death." However, the thief did not speak a word. The steward stripped him of his clothes and beat him with many stripes. As they ripped his clothes, they found much money hidden inside. So they said to him, "So, what are these?"

Immediately, the thief cried saying, "Master, I have sinned."

He admitted his theft before the multitude and confessed everything that he had done. He was then thrown in a dungeon, without food or water, and left to die.

Eulogios received all his money back and was exceedingly joyful. He gave sixty pounds of gold to the shrine and made a great feast for all the poor and sick people of the city. The money that Eulogios found with the thief amounted to five thousand pounds. After this, Eulogios besought the steward and the thief was set free. Eulogios gave the thief three pounds in gold and a new robe to wear. When the thief saw the compassion of Eulogios, he was touched and decided to give the three pounds to the shrine of Saint George. The thief was amazed at Saint George's miracle and how he had revealed the truth to the steward through a vision. Consequently, the thief vowed to serve the sick people until the day of his death. The thief kept his promise and Saint George received him favourably and forgave him his sins.

Saint George appeared to Eulogios by night and said to him, "God has heard your prayer and has accepted your alms. For this, he will show you great mercy. When you return to your house, you will find another ship which is greater than the one you had before. The ship will be laden with stores and wood. Take them to the city and build a shrine in my name. I will bless you and you shall not lack anything."

Eulogios returned to Antioch where he found the ship that Saint George had promised. He sent many charities to the poor and sick and he gave his first fruits to the church. He also built a shrine for Saint George where he ministered until the day of his death.

NINTH MIRACLE

During the reign of Diocletian, there was a certain general under his authority, whose name was Euchios. He was savage in appearance and exceedingly wicked in disposition. He was appointed with three thousand soldiers and sent into Egypt to overthrow all the churches and build idols instead. Euchios commanded that all Christians be bound and inflicted with great tortures. Many died as martyrs on the name of the Lord Jesus.

Awhile later, Diocletian told Euchios, "I know you are a prudent man as you perform all the decrees set out by the emperors. Rise up now, take soldiers and overthrow the shrine of Saint George for I cannot bear to hear the magic that occurs in that place. Many people are believing in this magic and are becoming Christians."

Euchios set out to Syria, with three thousand soldiers. He commanded his soldiers, saying, "Go destroy the shrine of Saint George. Then pull down all the churches, bind the Christians and cast them into prison. Punish them and inflict fearful sufferings on them and cut their heads with the sword."

The soldiers entered the city with swords, weapons, bows and arrows and the multitude was disturbed by this. Euchios held a staff in his hands and entered into the shrine of Saint George. When he went in, he saw a lamp burning with light. He said, "Look at this senseless thing. The sun can provide light, why do they need these lamps."

He smote the lamp with the staff in his hand and the lamp broke into small fragments. A piece of glass stuck to his head and oil spilt on his body. Every part of his body which the oil touched, became leprous. Euchios turned to his soldiers and said: "We have heard with our ears that there is a magician in this place, but today we have seen with our eyes." The soldiers marvelled at the power of Saint George who was capable of making Euchios leprous.

As Euchios left the shrine, his head became dizzy and he fell headlong on the ground. His whole body trembled and he was unable to stand. His soldiers carried him to their house where they ate and drank, but Euchios could not taste anything because his head was suffering great pain. In the evening, Euchios went to sleep and saw a vision. He saw a soldier, whose name was George, shoot an arrow into the air. The arrow stuck to Euchios' head and so he cried saying, "George, George."

Immediately, he awoke from his sleep.

Euchios was suffering greatly from the piece of glass in his head so he cried saying, "Let us go back to our country. I do not want to die in this foreign place."

The soldiers embarked on a ship and set sail to Antioch. Euchios' head suppurated and on the third day, he died. Within five days, his body became a mass of worms and so the soldiers took him and buried him in the sea. When the soldiers returned to Antioch, they told Diocletian about everything that had occurred at the shrine of Saint George. However, Diocletian did not believe them. He hardened his heart and said to the soldiers, "You are lying to me. I will go to the shrine myself and investigate. I will destroy the shrine and force all Christians to worship idols."

So Diocletian prepared an army and said, "Prepare yourself, O soldiers, for we are going to Syria to overthrow the shrine of the arch-sorcerer of the Galileans."

Immediately, Archangel Michael and Saint George came down from heaven and overturned the throne upon which emperor Diocletian sat. The golden pomegranates which were on the top of the throne struck his eyes and crushed his eyeballs.

Diocletian cried saying, "Woe is me, O my Lord. Woe is me. I have sinned. Forgive me. I have wrought great evil."

Archangel Michael replied saying, "You shall not be forgiven in this world or in the world to come. Your dominion will pass away and will be given to Constantine who is more excellent than you."

The multitude of soldiers and senators who were assembled in the royal presence, heard the words of Archangel Michael and greatly marvelled. Diocletian was cast from his throne and Constantine took over. Indeed Constantine loved God, loved charity and loved goodness.

Glory be to God forever, Amen.